The Ultimate Guide To Crochet Basics

Arnoldz .U Burtonn

The Advantages Of Crochet

A single needle with a hooked edge and yarn are used to create textiles when crocheting, a form of yarn art. Shawls, sweaters, socks, and other items can be made with crochet, just like knitting.

Initially, it was thought that knitting and crocheting were just hobbies for people with lots of free time. Making clothes for their loved ones was also regarded as a well-liked hobby for elderly people.

The trends did alter over time, though. Nowadays, people of all ages enjoy crocheting because it has so many possibilities. You did read that correctly. All ages can crochet.

Basically anything and everything can now be crocheted.

You can create a variety of items using just one stitch or a combination of several stitches once you dedicate yourself to learning at least three to four basic crochet stitching techniques.

You might feel the need to defend your hobby if crocheting is taking up an increasing amount of your time. There are many more factors than just these ten that make crocheting a fantastic way to spend your free time, but these are some of the best!

It relieves stress

Nothing can distract you from your worries like focusing on a pattern you enjoy while also using your hands steadily and enjoying the feel of the yarn. So if life is giving you lemons, grab your crocheting needles and hooks.

It alleviates depression

Crocheting is thought to help with more serious conditions like depression in addition to general stress and anxiety. Serotonin, the brain's natural anti-depressant, is released by the repetitive movements required for crocheting. In a survey of more than 3,000 knitters for the British Journal of Occupational Therapy, 81% of patients said they felt happier after working with yarn.

It benefits your body.

Crocheting has demonstrated health advantages in addition to being a mood enhancer because the small, repetitive movements required can keep your hands, arms, and fingers flexible and your eyes sharp. If you crochet a lot, consider ergonomically shaped hooks because they are easier on the joints.

It keeps the mind sharp.

The math-related aspects of crocheting, such as keeping track of your stitches, paying attention to the beginnings and ends of rows, and adding up pattern repetitions, all help to keep your thinking skills sharp, which many experts believe may prevent conditions like Alzheimer's.

It's original

When you create something that makes you or others happy, you will feel very satisfied. You will understand how unique that feeling is if you have ever made a truly amazing blanket or given someone a scarf and seen a look of appreciation on their face.

It supports tranquility and mindfulness.

Crocheting is regarded by the sizable mindfulness movement that has developed around coloring and relaxation methods as the ideal activity for enhancing mindfulness. Repeated crochet patterns are especially effective at fostering an open, mindful state. You can work your way toward inner peace by envisioning rows of single or double crocheting for straightforward blankets or scarves -- perhaps with variegated yarn to add some color interest without the interruption of changing yarns.

It boosts confidence

Crocheters can benefit from the simple act of completing a project because it can boost their self-esteem. No matter how big or small the task, finishing something from beginning to end can bring with it a sense of accomplishment and joy that cannot be understated. If you're just learning how to crochet, make this more doable by starting with projects that aren't as ambitious or by participating in a CAL (crochet along project).

It benefits others.

Giving back to your community is always fulfilling, and crocheting allows you to do this. Make premature baby clothes if a hospital is close by. These items are hard to find in stores and can be very reassuring for both children and parents. Likewise, children's wards appreciate receiving donations of crocheted toys. On their website, Knitted Knockers offers a crochet pattern for their prosthetic breasts, which are made for cancer patients.

It builds a community.

Look out for crochet gatherings in your area because it's great to meet others who share your interests. Why not establish one if it doesn't already? A yarn shop, a coffee shop, or your local library are all excellent options for meeting locations.

It aids in breaking bad habits.

Crocheting could be a big help if you've had trouble quitting smoking, if you drink a little too much, or if you always reach for the snacks. Keeping your hands occupied with something constructive and positive can help you break bad habits and divert your attention from unhelpful worries so that you can focus on something constructive instead.

It is a convenient, orderly pastime that you can make as challenging or simple as you like.

With just a ball of yarn and a hook, you can crochet anywhere, unlike when hunting or fishing for large game. You can crochet at any stage of life and make things for family, friends, and yourself that have something special added to them, with a little of your own inspiration and lots of love. You can crochet while working or while watching TV on a boring train commute.

Crocheting increases self-esteem because it's productive.

Everyone wants to feel useful and productive, and creating a project to give as a gift or sell at a craft fair can help us achieve that.

Even though we don't craft for attention alone, a few external compliments—such as when someone buys your finished product or when the recipient of a gift wears the crocheted hat you made all winter—can help us develop the self-esteem we require.

Crocheting transforms a pastime into a business.

You might not be aware that you can sell your crocheted artwork online. You can also sign up for Facebook groups that let you buy and sell handmade goods.

Sincere to say, crocheting has a lot more advantages than those already mentioned.

Crocheting has a number of advantages for the mind, body, and emotions in addition to being a traditional skill and an undeniable means of creativity and expression.

If you already knit or crochet, we hope that this blog will keep you interested in this fulfilling hobby.

If you're just getting started, we hope this blog will inspire you to continue on your journey.

Contents

Wearable Accessories 1
Hairpin Lace Pirate Toque Pattern 2
    About: 2
    Materials Needed: 2
    Abbreviations Used: 2
    Pattern: 2
Vintage Skull Cap 5
    About: 5
    Materials needed: 5
    Abbreviations Used: 5
    Pattern: 6
Sport Scarf 8
    About: 8
    Materials needed: 8
    Abbreviations Used: 8
    Pattern: 9
Scarf Collar 10
    About: 10
    Materials Needed: 10
    Abbreviations Used: 10
    Pattern: 10
Striped Poncho 13
    About: 13
    Materials Needed: 13
    Abbreviations Used: 13
    Pattern: 14
Simple Poncho 16
    About: 16
    Materials Needed: 16
    Abbreviations Used: 16
    Pattern: 16
Home Decor 18

Draped Curtains With Pom Poms 19
    About: 19
    Materials Needed: 19
    Abbreviations Used: 19
Curtain. 20
Tie-back 20
Ball Trimming. 20
Cute Cubed Coaster Set With Matching Centerpiece 21
    About: 21
    Materials Needed: 21
    Abbreviations Used: 21
Doilies 22
Edgings 22
Centerpiece 22
Striped Circle Coasters With A Scalloped Edge 23
    About: 23
    Materials Needed: 23
    Abbreviations Used: 23
To Make The Bottom. 23
To Make The Edging. 24
Italian Table Place Mats 25
    About: 25
    Materials Needed: 25
    Abbreviations Used: 25
To Make The Place Mat. 26
Four Pointed Star Potholder 27
    About: 27
    Materials Needed: 27
    Abbreviations Used: 27
    Pattern: 27
Points 28
Border 28
Comfy Oblong Pillow (Great For The Patio!) 30

- About: 30
  - Materials Needed: 30
  - Abbreviations Used: 30
  - Pattern: 30
- Blankets And Afghans 32
- Cozy Stripes Mile A Minute Afghan 33
  - About: 33
  - Materials Needed: 33
  - Abbreviations Used: 33
- First Large Strip: 34
- Second Large Strip 35
- Rivers That Ripple Afghan 36
  - About: 36
  - Materials Needed: 36
  - Abbreviations Used: 36
  - Pattern: 37
- Edging 38
- Geometric Triangle Afghan 39
  - About: 39
  - Materials Needed: 39
  - Abbreviations Used: 39
- Afghan Stitch 40
  - Row 1: 40
  - Row 2: 40
  - Decrease: 40
  - Pattern: 40
- Border 41
- Scotch Plaid Woven Afghan 42
  - About: 42
  - Materials Needed: 42
  - Abbreviations Used: 42
  - Pattern: 43
- Weaving. 43

Two-Tone Blocked Afghan 45
    About: 45
    Materials Needed: 45
    Abbreviations Used: 45
One Square 46
Border 46
Bulky Cozy Baby Blanket 47
    About: 47
    Materials Needed: 47
    Abbreviations Used: 47
Center 47
Border 48
Carriage Cover Baby Afghan 50
    About: 50
    Materials Needed: 50
    Abbreviations Used: 50
    Pattern: 51
Border: 51
Patterns With A Purpose 53
Moss Stitch Dish Cloth Pattern 54
    About: 54
    Materials Needed: 54
    Abbreviations Used: 54
    Pattern: 54
Two-Toned Toaster Cover Pattern 56
    About: 56
    Materials Needed: 56
    Abbreviations Used: 56
    Pattern: 56
Gusset 57
Weaving 57
Frilly Edged Candy Dish 58
    About: 58

Materials Needed:	58
Abbreviations Used:	58
Pattern:	58
To Stiffen Your Bowl:	60
Grandma's Traditional Toilet Seat Cover	61
About:	61
Materials Needed:	61
Abbreviations Used:	61
Pattern:	62
Border	62
Oval Bath Mat	64
About:	64
Materials Needed:	64
Abbreviations Used	64
Pattern:	64
Bumble Bee Striped Oven Mitt Pattern	66
About:	66
Materials Needed:	66
Abbreviations Used:	66
Mitt	67
Thumb	67
Advanced Patterns	69
Three Little Bears Amigurumi Pattern	70
About:	70
Materials Needed:	70
Abbreviations Used:	70
Pattern:	70
Body:	70
Sweetheart Toy Puppy	75
About:	75
Materials Needed:	75
Abbreviations Used:	75
Pattern:	75

- A Modern Crocheted Apron 80
  - About: 80
  - Materials Needed: 80
  - Abbreviations Used: 80
- WAISTBAND 80
- Hot Springs Bedspread 82
  - About: 82
  - Materials Needed: 82
  - Abbreviations Used: 82
  - Pattern: 83
- Chain Mesh Designer Gloves 85
  - About: 85
  - Materials Needed: 85
  - Abbreviations Used: 85
- Forefinger, Middle Finger, Ring Finger and Little Finger 85
- Thumb. 86
- Palm. 86
- Cuff. 87

Chapter 1:
Wearable Accessories

A great way to combine practicality with fun is to create crocheted wearable accessories! With crochet, there are so many different accessories you can create for yourself that are also wearable. For example, hats, scarves, and ponchos! These patterns can keep you warm, help you look stylish, and offer you something to be proud of having made for yourself. They also make wonderful gifts for loved ones, especially since all of these patterns can easily be made into one-size-fits most pattern. Customize your patterns with the favorite colors of your recipients, whether it be yourself of someone else, and you are sure to have a wonderful piece that you can be proud of having made yourself! The bonus? These are all incredibly easy patterns that you can work up, regardless of your skill level.

Hairpin Lace Pirate Toque Pattern

Beginner/Easy

About:

The hairpin toque pattern is a beautiful toque that uses a tassel to offer a flair of style to the top of the toque.

Materials Needed:

4 oz. bulky weight yarn in your color of choice. Hairpin staple 2" wide. Crochet hook size F.

Abbreviations Used:

Chain (Ch)
Single Crochet (Sc)
Slip Stitch (Sl St)

Pattern:

For the Hairpin Lace: Make a loop at the end of your yarn and insert 1 prong of hairpin staple in the loop. Wind your yarn around the right prong of the hairpin staple. Yarn over hook, draw through loop, keeping the loop at the center of the staple. Drop the loop, turn the staple one half turn to the left, then pick up the dropped loop at the center and insert the hook through the top part of the loop on the left hand prong. Pull a loop through, there should now be 2 loops on your hook. Yarn over, and pull it through both of the loops on your hook, completing one Sc. Repeat until there are 64 loops on each side of your staple. Cut the yarn. Work another strip of hairpin lace in the same manner.

Round 1: Attach bulky yarn in 1st 2 loops of 1st strip of hairpin lace. *Ch 2, keep the twist in the loops and Sc through next 2 loops of hairpin lace. Go through both loops at the same time. *Repeat from* to * across the stip. Ch 2, join to 1st Sc with Sl St. (This makes lower edge of your hat).

Round 2: Ch 1, working through back loop of stitches only, 1 Sl St in each Sc and Ch across. Join with Sl St.

Round 3: Working through back loop of stitches only, 1 Sl St in each Sl St. Join. Cut yarn. Sew center of hairpin lace together.

Round 4: Attach bulky yarn in first 2 loops on the opposite side of the same strip. *Ch 2, keep the twist in the loops and Sc through next 2 loops of hairpin lace. Go through both loop´s at the same time. *Repeat from * to * around. Ch 2. Join with Sl St.

Round 5: Join strips as follows: Sl St in next Ch 2 space. Ch 1, Sc through first 2 loops of second strip. Ch 1, Sl St in next Ch 2 space of first strip. *Ch 1, Sc through next 2 loops of 2nd strip, Ch 1, Sl St in next Ch 2 space of first strip. * Repeat from * to * around, ending with Ch 1. Join with Sl St. Cut the yarn. Work another strip of hairpin lace.

Round 6: Attach bulky yarn through first three hoops at the top of the second strip. *Ch 2, Sc, through next 3 loops of hairpin lace. * Repeat from * to * around, Ch 2 and join. Work another strip of hairpin lace.

Round 7: Attach bulky yarn through first three loops at the top of the third strip of hairpin lace. * Ch 2, Sc through next 3 loops of hairpin lace. * Repeat from * to * around. Ch 2, Join with Sl St.

Round 8: Sl St into Ch 2 space and join fourth strip to third strip the same way you did the first two strip. Cut the yarn. Attach bulky yarn though the first four loops at the top of the fourth strip of hairpin lace. *Ch 1, Sc through next 4 loops of hairpin lace. * Repeat from * to * around, Ch 1, Join with Sl St. Cut yarn with a long tail, then thread the yarn through a needle and draw the top of your hat together. Keep the tail long.

For the Tassel: Wind yarn around 4¼ inch cardboard 25 times. Use a small piece of yarn to tie end so all of the loops are tied together. Cut the yarn on the opposite end of the cardboard length. Tie it again approximately ¾" down from the first knot. Trim the tassel evenly, then sew it on to the tip of your hat. Turn the top over about 4" and sew the tassel to the side of your hat so it stays in place.

Vintage Skull Cap

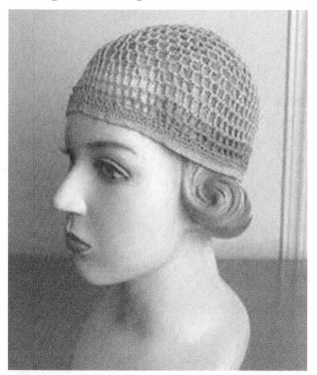

Beginner/Easy

About:

This skull cap is a petite cap that just fits over the top of your head as a way to keep you warm, while also looking stylish. It is an excellent hat or toque for anyone who is looking for something that is not too bulky, and that will still serve excellent warmth.

Materials needed:

3 weight yarn in 3 different colors designated as A, B, and C. Crochet hook size D.

Abbreviations Used:

Chain (Ch)

Single Crochet (Sc)
Slip Stitch (Sl St)

Pattern:

Pattern starts at the tip. Ch 10 with color C.

Round 1: Sc in 3rd Ch from hook. Sc in each of the next 6 Ch spaces. 10 Sc in last Ch. Sc in 10th Sc from hook. Have the point forward, toward you. 2 Sc in each Sc around until you have 21 Sc total in the round.

Round 2: Sc in each Sc around. Sl St to join.

Round 3: *Sc in next Sc, 2 Sc in next Sc (one increase made.) *Repeat from * to * around. Sl St to join.

Round 4: Sc in each Sc around. Sl St to join.

Round 5: *2 Sc in next Sc, Sc in each of next 2 Sc. * Repeat from * to * around. Sl St to join.

Round 6: Sc in each Sc around. Sl St to join.

Round 7: *2 Sc in next Sc, Sc in each of next 3 Sc. * Repeat from * to * around. Sl St to join.

Round 8: Sc in each Sc around. Sl St to join. Drop color C to back of work.

Round 9: Attach color A. Sc in each Sc around. Sl St to join. Drop color A to back of work.

Round 10: Attach color B. Sc in each next 2 Sc. *2 Sc in next Sc. Sc in each of next 4 Sc. * Repeat from * to * around. Sl St to join.

Round 11: Sc in each Sc around. Sl St to join.

Round 12: Sc in each of the next 3 Sc. *2 Sc in next Sc, Sc in each of next 7 Sc. * Repeat from * to * around. Sl St to join.

Round 13: Attach color A. Sc in each Sc around. Sl St to join. Drop color A to back of work.

Round 14: Pick up color C. Work Sc in next Sc. *2 Sc in next Sc. Sc in each of next 5 Sc. * Repeat from * to * around. Sl St to join.

Round 15: Sc in each Sc around. Sl St to join. Drop color C to back of work.

Round 16: Pick up color A. Sc in each of next 3 Sc. *2 Sc in next Sc. Sc in each of next 7 Sc. *Repeat from * to * around. Sl St to join. Drop A to the back.

Round 17: Attach color B. Sc in each Sc around. Sl St to join.

Round 18: Sc in each of next 3 Sc. *2 Sc in next Sc. Sc in each of next 7 Sc. * Repeat * to * around. Sl St to join. Drop color B to the back.

Remaining Rounds: With color A, Sc in each Sc until work measures 6 ½" from tip to edge of work.

Final Round: Sc in base of each Sc around. Sl St to join. Cut off and fasten in your end.

Sport Scarf

Beginner/Easy

About:

This scarf offers both style and functionality, being that it is a chunky warm scarf that is sure to keep you cozy during the cooler months. Although this scarf is big and bold, it is an incredibly easy pattern to create. You will love designing this piece for yourself, or a loved one!

Materials needed:

7 skeins of 4 weight yarn. 5 skeins of color A, 2 skeins of color B. Crochet hook size E.

Abbreviations Used:

Chain (Ch)

Pattern:

Ch 61.

The row: *Wrap yarn around hook, insert hook into next stitch, wrap yarn around hook, pull yarn through, wrap around hook, pull it through all three loops on the hook. One loop remaining. *Repeat * to * across. Ch 1, turn.

Complete the row to create the following pattern:

17 rows of color A

2 rows of color B

3 rows of color A

3 rows of color B

3 rows of color A

4 rows of color B

50 inches of color A

4 rows of color B

3 rows of color A

3 rows of color B

3 rows of color A

2 rows of color B

17 rows of color A

To create your fringe, cut 8 inch strands of color A and color B yarn. Use 3 strands of color A and 3 strands of color B, fold them in half, insert the fold into a stitch on the end of your scarf and pull the ends through the loop. Pull tight and repeat on every 3rd stitch until you have fringe across both ends.

Scarf Collar

Beginner/Easy.

About:

This scarf collar creates a beautiful kerchief-style scarf that will provide both warmth and style to any outfit you are wearing. Because of its smaller size, this pattern works up much faster. You can easily create it in as little as one single afternoon!

Materials Needed:

3 weight yarn, one ball in color A and one ball in color B. Crochet hook in size D. Two snap fasteners.

Abbreviations Used:

Chain (Ch)
Slip Stitch (Sl St)
Single Crochet (Sc)
Double Crochet (Dc)

Pattern:

In Color A, Ch 19. Turn.

Row 1: Sl St in 7th Ch from hook. *Ch 3, skip 2 Ch stitches, Sl St in the next stitch. *Repeat * to – 3 more times. Ch 6, turn.

Row 2: Dc in 4th Ch from hook. Skip Sl St and Ch loop. Dc in next Sl St space. * Ch 3, Dc in Dc just made, Dc in next Sl St. Repeat from * to * 3 more times. Make last Dc in 3rd Ch of turning Ch. (5 patterns made.) Ch 3, turn.

Row 3: Dc in 1st Dc, *Ch 3, Dc in Dc just made, Dc in next Dc from previous row. * Repeat from * to * 4 more times. Ch 6, turn.

Row 4: Dc in 4th Ch from hook, skip 1st Dc of previous row, Dc in next Dc, *Ch 3, in Dc just made, Dc in next Dc from previous row. *Repeat from * to * 3 more times. Ch 2, Sc in Dc just made, Dc in turning Ch 3 space after row 2 (an increase has been made.) Ch 5, turn.

Row 5: Sc in 3rd Ch from hook. Skip 1st Dc of previous row, Dc in next Dc, *Ch 3, Dc in Dc just made. Dc in next Dc of previous row. *Repeat from * to * 4 more times. Ch 6, turn.

Row 6: Dc in 4th Ch from hook. Skip 1st Dc, Dc in next Dc from previous row. *Ch 3, Dc in just made. Dc in next Dc. *Repeat from * to * 4 more times. Ch 3, turn 1 pattern has been increased on the side that will be on the neck edge.

Repeat 3rd, 4th, 5th and 6th rows in order, till there are 22 patterns in the row. For every repetition of these 4 rows, repeat the portion between the *'s one additional time care for increases.

Next, work 10 rows straight. Make Ch 3 loops to finish the outer and neck edges of collar.

Trimming: Attach color B at the right-angle corner, and work along last row as follows: Ch 6, Dc in 4th Ch from hook, Dc in place where Ch 6 started. *Dc in next Dc, Ch 3, Dc in Dc just made, make another Dc in the same Dc from previous row. *Repeat from * to * until you reach the corner. In the corner, make 2 patterns, then continue along other side. At next corner break and fasten thread. Attach color B in 4th row from last, and work another trimming row, parallel to first trimming row. Drape around neck as illustrated and sew on snap fasteners. Sew on buttons with color B.

Striped Poncho

Beginner/Easy.

About:

This striped poncho creates a beautiful poncho that will drape over any figure. It is warm, stylish, and makes for a wonderful present for yourself or someone else. Although this is a larger project and it will require more commitment from you, it is not a project that will require a large amount of skill. Instead, it allows your beginner-level skills to be put to work to make something truly magnificent. This poncho will take a few days to make, at least, but once you are done you will be proud of the piece you have created.

Materials Needed:

4 weight yarn in 6 colors. 14 balls of main color, 3 balls of color A, 2 balls of color B, 3 balls of color C, 3 balls of color D, 3 balls of color E. Crochet hook in size I.

Abbreviations Used:

Chain (Ch)
Slip Stitch (Sl St)
Triple Crochet (Tr)

Cluster yarn (yarn over hook, draw up a loop in next stitch, yarn over hook and draw through first 2 loops on hooks, 3 times in same stitch. Yarn over hook and drawn through all 4 loops on the hook, ch 1 to fasten.)

Pattern:

Worked in one piece, starting at neck edge. With main color, Ch 96. Join with Sl St to form a ring.

Round 1: Ch 4, skip 1 Ch 1 Tr in next Ch space, (Ch 1, skip 1 Ch 1 Tr in next Ch space.) 9 times *Ch 2, skip 1 Ch, (Cluster, Ch 2, Cluster) in next Ch space, Ch 2, skip 1 Ch space, 1 Tr in next Ch space, (Ch 1, skip 1 Ch, 1 Tr in next Ch) 10 times. *Repeat from * to * twice. Ch 2, skip 1 Ch space, (Cluster, Ch 2, Cluster) in next Ch space, Ch 2, skip 1 Ch, Sl St in 3rd Ch at beginning of round, fasten off.

Round 2: Join in color A in any Ch 2 space after a Cluster group. Ch 4, 1 Tr in next Ch 1 space, * (Ch 1, 1 Tr) in each Ch 1 space to corner, Ch 1, 1 Tr in Ch2 space, Ch 2, (Cluster, Ch 2, Cluster) in Ch 2 space between Cluster, Ch 2, 1 Tr in Ch 2 space. *Repeat from * to * 3 times, omitting 1 Tr at end of last repeat. Sl St in 3rd Ch at beginning of round, fasten off.

Round 3: Join in color B in any Ch 2 space after a Cluster group, Ch 4, 1 Tr in same space. *(Ch 1, 1 Tr) in each Ch 1 space to corner, Ch 1, 1 Tr in Ch 2 space, (Cluster, Ch 2, Cluster) in Ch 2 space between Cluster, Ch 2, (1 Tr, Ch 1, 1 Tr) in space. *Repeat from * to * 3 times, omitting (1 Tr, 1 Ch, 1 Tr) at end of last repetition. Sl St in 3rd Ch at beginning of round, fasten off.

Repeat 2nd and 3rd rounds working in 1 round stripes of color B, main color, color C, main color, color D, main color, color E, main color, color A, main color, until work measures 22 inches. Finish with an M stripe.

For the Fringe: Wind main color around a piece of cardboard 4 inches wide and cut the yarn along one side. With wrong side facing and using 4 strands of yarn, fold yarn in half and draw loop through a Ch space at the lower edge of your poncho, pull ends through loop and tighten. Repeat in each Ch space around lower edge, working 2 knots in each 2 Ch spaces next to corners and 3 knots in corner spaces.

Simple Poncho

Advanced.

About:

This simple poncho is a beautiful piece that uses one solid color to create a stylish design. The decorative fringe pieces on the end add to the aesthetic of this pattern, making it even more enjoyable to make, and to wear. Because of the motifs used for the pattern, you will notice this pattern is more advanced in nature.

Materials Needed:

4 weight yarn. 44 balls in main color, 37 for the poncho and 7 for the fringe. Size G crochet hook.

Abbreviations Used:

Chain (Ch)
Slip Stitch (Sl St)
Triple Crochet (Tr)

Pattern:

Chain 132. Join with Sl St to form a ring.

Round 1: Ch 5, 3 Tr in same Ch as Sl St, * (Ch 2, skip 2 ch spaces, 1 Tr in each of next 3 Ch spaces) 6 times. Ch 2, skip 2 Ch spaces, (3 Tr, Ch 2, 3 Tr) in next Ch space (corner), * Repeat from * to * twice. (Ch 2, skip 2 ch spaces, 1 Tr in each of next 3 Ch spaces) 6 times, Ch 2, skip 2 ch spaces, 2 Tr in same Ch as Sl St, Sl St in 3rd Ch of 5 Ch loop.

Round 2: Sl St in Ch 2 space, Ch 5, 3 Tr in corner space, * (Ch 2, 3 Tr) in each Ch 2 space to corner space, Ch 2, (3 Tr, Ch 2, 3 Tr) in corner space. * Repeat from * to * twice. (Ch 2, 3 Tr) in each Ch 2 space to corner space. 2 Tr in corner space, Sl St in 3rd Ch of 5 Ch loop.

Repeat round 2 35 times. Fasten off.

MOTIFS (Make 48)

Chain 6, join with a Sl St to form a ring.

Round 1: (Ch 5, 1 Dc in ring) 4 times.

Round 2: Sl St in Ch 5 loop. Ch 3, (yarn over hook, draw up a loop in same Ch loop, yarn over hook and draw through 2 loops on hook) twice, yarn over hook and draw through all 3 loops on hook, Ch 2, Cluster in same Ch 5 loop, Ch 3, (Cluster, Ch 2, Cluster, Ch 3) in each Ch 5 loop, Sl St in 3rd Ch at beginning of round.

Round 3: Sl St to Ch 2 space, Sl St in space, Ch 3, 2 Tr in Ch 2 space. *Ch 2, (3 Tr, Ch 3, 3 Tr) in Ch 3 loop, Ch 2, 3 Tr in Ch 2 space. * Repeat from * to * twice. Ch 2, (3 Tr, Ch 3, 3 Tr) in Ch 3 loop, Ch 2, Sl St in 3rd Ch at beginning of round.

Round 4: Sl St to Ch 2 space, Sl St in space, Ch 3, 2 Tr in ch 2 space. *Ch2, (3 Tr, Ch 3, 3 Tr) in Ch 3 loop, (2 Ch, 3 Tr in Ch 2 space) twice. *Repeat from * to * twice, Ch 2, (3 Tr, Ch 3, 3 Tr) in Ch 3 loop, Ch 2, 3 Tr in Ch 2 space, Ch 2, Sl St in 3rd Ch at beginning of round. Fasten off.

Chapter 2:
Home Decor

Making home decor is an excellent way to showcase your creative talents. Adorning your house with homemade curtains, doilies, or other home decor allows you to take pride in your creations and put them on display for everyone to see. These gifts also make for wonderful housewarming presents for friends or loved ones who may be moving into their new homes. Be sure to make them in a color that matches the color scheme of the room they will be displayed in!

Draped Curtains With Pom Poms

Beginner/Easy.

About:

This curtain is a simple pattern for any beginner to make. It provides an elegant, vintage look to any room it is added to. Unlike some curtains, this one should be fairly sheer, meaning it will continue to let beautiful light through, while also giving you something stunning to look at. You will certainly be proud of this project when you are done!

Materials Needed:

3 weight yarn. 38 balls of any color you desire. Crochet hook in size D.

Abbreviations Used:

Chain (Ch)
Slip Stitch (Sl St)
Double Crochet (Dc)
Triple Crochet (Tr)

Pattern:

Curtain.

Starting at the bottom of your curtain, make a chain that is about 4 yards long.

Row 1: Dc in 8th Ch from hook, *Ch 2, skip 2 Ch spaces, Dc in next Ch. * Repeat from * to * across. Ch 10 (to count as Tr, Tr and Ch 2). Turn.

Row 2: Tr, Tr (thread over 4 times) in next Dc, *Ch2, Tr, Tr in next Dc. *Repeat from * to * across, making last Tr, Tr in 3rd stitch of turning chain. Ch 5, turn.

Row 3: *Dc in next Tr, Tr, Ch 2. *Repeat from * to * across, making last Dc in 3rd stitch of turning chain. Ch 10, turn.

The last 2 rows constitute the pattern. Work in pattern until piece measures 2 ¾ yards long, or length desired.

Tie-back

Make a chain about 18 inches long. Work in curtain pattern for 5 rows, starting and ending with Dc space rows.

Ball Trimming.

Cut 2 pieces of cardboard, 1 ½ inches in diameter each. At the center of each piece, cut a ½ inch hole. Place the 2 pieces together. Cut 12 strands of thread, about 4 yards long each. Wind them around the cardboard circle until the center hole is completely filled in. Cut around the edges of the yarn, leaving the center hold still filled in. Take a small piece of yarn and tie it around the center pieces. Remove the cardboard and trim evenly. Sew balls 6 inches apart on side and lower edges.

Cute Cubed Coaster Set With Matching Centerpiece

Beginner.

About:

This coaster set will make 6 coasters, with each coaster being approximately 5 inches squared. The matching centerpiece will be approximately 7 inches square, and works beautifully under a bouquet of flowers, or a delightful meal you are serving to your guests.

Materials Needed:

5 balls of lace weight yarn. Crochet hook size C.

Abbreviations Used:

Chain (Ch)
Slip Stitch (Sl St)
Single Crochet (Sc)
Double Crochet (Dc)

Pattern:

Doilies

(Make 6)

Ring 1: Starting at the center, Ch 10. Join with Sl St.

Round 1: Ch 1, 2 Dc in ring, (Ch 3, 3 Dc in ring) 7 times. Ch 3, Sl St to 3rd stitch of Ch 3 space. Fasten off.

Second ring: Ch 10; join. Ch 3, 2 Dc in ring, Ch 1, Sl St in corresponding Ch 3 of first ring, Ch 1, 3 Dc back into second ring. Complete as for 1st ring.

Make 8 x8 rings, joining to adjacent rings as 2nd was joined to 1st, leaving one Ch 2 loop free between joining spaces.

Edgings

Round 1: Attach thread to center Ch 3 loop of ring to the right of corner ring. *(Ch 5, Sc in 3rd Ch from hook – a pattern made) twice. Ch 1, skip 1 loop of corner ring, Sc in next loop, Ch 2, pattern, Ch 1, skip 1 loop, Sc in next loop of corner ring. (Ch 2, pattern, Ch 2, pattern, Ch 1, Sc in center loop of next ring) 6 times. * Repeat * to * around, ending with Sc in same place where thread was joined.

Round 2: Sl St to center Ch (between pattern's) of next loop, *Ch 2, pattern, Ch 2, pattern, Ch 1, Sc in next Sc, Ch 2, pattern, Ch 2, pattern, Ch 1, Sc between next 2 patterns of corner loop, Ch 2, pattern, Ch 2, patter, Ch 1, Sc in next Sc, (Ch 2, pattern, Ch 2, pattern, Ch 1, Sc in next loop between patterns) 7 times. * Repeat * to * around. Join. Fasten off.

Centerpiece

Work as for doilies but make 11 x 11 rings. Finish as for doilies. Block to 7" squared.

Striped Circle Coasters With A Scalloped Edge

Advanced.

About:

These striped circular coasters have a beautiful scalloped edge that make them look absolutely delightful. They work wonderfully as everyday coasters, or as a set that can be used during special parties, or when you have beloved guests over.

Materials Needed:

4 weight yarn, 4 balls. 2 balls of color A, 2 balls of color B. Crochet hook size H.

Abbreviations Used:

Chain (Ch)
Slip Stitch (Sl St)
Single Crochet (Sc)
Double Crochet (Dc)

Pattern:

To Make The Bottom.

Round 1: Starting at center with color A, Ch 4. 11 Dc in 4th Ch from hook. Sl St in top stitch of starting chain.

Round 2: Drop color A, attach color B, Ch 1, Sc in same place as Sl St, *2 Sc in next stitch, Sc in next stitch. * Repeat from * to * around. Join.

Round 3: Drop color B, pick up color A. Ch 3, Dc in each stitch around, increasing 12 Dc evenly around. To increase a Dc, make 2 Dc in 1 stitch.

Round 4: Drop color A, pick up color B, Ch 1. Sc in each stitch around, increasing 6 Sc evenly around.

Repeat the rounds 3 and 4 alternately until piece measures about ¼ inch larger all around than bottom of glass, ending with a round 3.

To Make The Edging.

Round 1: Drop color A and pick up color B. Turn and make Sc in back loop of each stitch around. Join.

Round 2: Drop color B, pick up color A. Sc in same place as Sl St. *Ch 5, 3 Dc where last Sc was made, skip 3 Sc, Sc in next Sc. * Repeat from * to * around. Join. Cut off color A.

Round 3: Pick up color B, *5 Sc in Ch 5 loop, Sc in next 3 Dc. * Repeat from * to * around. Join and break off.

Attach color B and, working over free loops of last Dc round of the Bottom, work a second edging as follows:

Round 1: Sc in each stitch around, increased by 8 Sc evenly around. Join.

Round 2: Same as round 2 of 1st edging, skipping 2 (instead of 3) stitches. Join and break off. Complete as for 1st edging.

Italian Table Place Mats

Beginner/Easy.

About:

These gorgeous place mats are a surefire way to brighten up your table. They take hardly any time to work up, and once they are designed they offer beautiful texture to an already stunning table display. Bring them out for everyday use, or use fancier colors and more delicate fibers for fancy luncheons or dinner parties!

Materials Needed:

4 weight yarn. 2 balls color A, 2 balls color B, 2 balls color C, 2 balls color D, 2 balls color E. Crochet hook in size H. 1/3 yard of natural colored linen. This is enough for 4 place mats, each of which will measure 13 ½ by 10 ½ inches.

Abbreviations Used:

Chain (Ch)
Slip Stitch (Sl St)
Single Crochet (Sc)

Pattern:

To Make The Place Mat.

Cut linen to measure 8 by 12 inches. Make a narrow hem.

Attach color A along 1 edge. Sc over hem, *Ch 1, Sc over hem. * Repeat fro * to * making Sc's about 1/8 inch apart. At corners make 3 Sc in same space, with a Ch 1 between each Sc. Ch 1 and join with Sl St to 1st stitch, Ch 1.

Row 1: *Sc over Ch 1 space, Ch 1. *Repeat from * to * around. At corners Ch 3 instead of Ch 1. Join with Sl St to 1st stitch of the row. Ch 1.

Row 2: *Sc over Ch 1 space, Ch 1. *Repeat from * to * around. At corner make 3 Sc's with a Ch 1 between each, over Ch 3 loops.

Alternate rows 2 and 3 for the entire mat, working in this pattern: 3 rows of color A, 1 row of color B, 3 rows of color C, 1 row of color B, 3 rows of color D, 1 row of color B, 3 rows of color E, 1 row of color B. The place mat will be finished with a row of color A.

Four Pointed Star Potholder

Advanced

About:

This four pointed star potholder is a beautiful crochet pattern that combines beginner level stitches with a more advanced design, to create a wonderful pattern for you to step up into if you are ready to advance beyond beginner patterns. This potholder can be used to lift hot pots out of a warm oven, or to rest them on your counter or table without wrecking your surface.

Materials Needed:

3 weight yarn, 4 balls. 2 in color A, 2 in color B. Crochet hook in size D.

Abbreviations Used:

Chain (Ch)
Slip Stitch (Sl St)
Single Crochet (Sc)

Pattern:

Use double thread therefore. Starting at center with color A, Ch 2.

Round 1: 8 Sc in 2nd Ch from hook. Join with Sl St to first Sc.

Round 2: 2 Sc in each Sc around (16 Sc). Join and cut off.

Round 3: Attach color B, Ch 1, 2 Sc in same place as thread was attached. *Sc in next 3 Sc, 3 Sc in next Sc (corner). * Repeat from * to * around, ending with Sc in same place as first 2 Sc were made. Join.

Rounds 4 and 5: Ch 1, 2 Sc in same place as Sl St. *Sc in each Sc to center Sc of next 3 Sc group, 3 Sc in next Sc. * Repeat from * to * around, ending the round as before. Drop color B.

Round 6: Attach color A and work the same as you did in round 5.

Rounds 7 and 8: Pick up color B, with B repeat round 5. Join and cut off.

Round 9: Pick up color A and repeat round 5.

Points

Row 1: Sc in each Sc across to center Sc of next 3 Sc group. Ch 1, turn.

Row 2: Work off 2 Sc as 1 Sc (1 Sc decreased.) Sc in each Sc across. Ch 1, turn.

Repeat 2nd row until all stitches are worked off. Cut off. Attach color A to center Sc of 2 Sc group and complete another point as before. Work remaining two points in same way.

Border

Round 1: Attach color B and Sc closely around, making 3 Sc at tip of each point. Join, drop color B.

Round 2: Attach color A and Sc in each Sc around, making 3 Sc in center Sc of each 3 Sc group. Join and cut off.

Round 3: Pick up color B and repeat round 2.

Comfy Oblong Pillow (Great For The Patio!)

Beginner/Easy.

About:

This simple oblong cushion is wonderful for back support, or for a small cushion to rest your head on when you are relaxing. Make it with a durable cotton so it can be safely used on the patio, without being damaged by the weather! Or, make it out of a fiber like pure wool or alpaca fiber for a designer piece for your home.

Materials Needed:

3 weight yarn. 4 balls of color A, 2 balls of color B. Crochet hook size C.

Abbreviations Used:

Chain (Ch)
Slip Stitch (Sl St)
Single Crochet (Sc)
Double Crochet (Dc)

Pattern:

Starting at narrow edge with color A, create a chain 16 inches long.

Row 1: Working with color A over a stand of color B, Sc in 2nd Ch from hook, *Working over color A with color B, Sc in next Ch. Working over color B with color A, Sc in next Ch. *Repeat from * to * across until the row measures 13 inches, ending with a Sc in color A. Ch 3, turn.

Row 2: Working over color B, skip first Sc, Dc in front loop of each Sc across. Ch 1, turn.

Row 3: Working over color B with color A, make Sc in first Dc, *Working over color A with color B, Sc in next Dc, working over color B with color A, Sc in next Dc. *Repeat from * to * across. Ch 3. Turn.

Repeat rows 2 and 3 alternately until piece measures length of your desired pillow, ending with a Sc row.

Cut off color B. With color A, Sc closely around, making 3 Sc in each corner. Join and cut off. Weave in your ends.

Chapter 3:
Blankets And Afghans

Blankets and afghans are a wonderful way to get into crocheting. With these patterns, you are generally following simple steps that are repeated throughout the entire project. On easier blankets, these steps include basic crochet stitches, while on more challenging projects they will feature complex stitches. This may sound like they are too challenging to do, however they are actually an excellent way to help advance your skills based on the fact that there is a lot of repetition. Once you understand how the pattern works, you simply repeat it for the entire project and before you know it you have mastered these new stitches! In this chapter, we will cover a variety of beginner and advanced blankets and afghans so you can begin to expand your skills while making beautiful projects at the same time.

Cozy Stripes Mile A Minute Afghan

Easy.

About:

This cozy stripes afghan is known as a "mile a minute" afghan because it is crocheted in stripes, and then those stripes are sewn together to create the entire blanket. The final product is 62 inches by 75 inches, making it a wonderfully large afghan that is excellent for snuggling up with.

Materials Needed:

Eight colors of 4 weight yarn: 17 x 1 oz skeins in color A, 17 x 1 oz skeins in color B, 17 x 1 oz skeins in color C, 11 x 1 oz skeins in color D, 11 x 1 oz skeins in color E, 11 x 1 oz skeins in color F, 9 x 1 oz skeins in color G, and 6 x 1 oz skeins in color H. Crochet hook in J.

Abbreviations Used:

Chain (Ch)
Single Crochet (Sc)
Slip Stitch (Sl St)

Pattern:

First Large Strip:

Starting at short end, with color A, Ch 9.

Row 1: Insert hook in 2nd Ch from hook and draw up a loop. Draw up a loop in each Ch stitch across, retaining all loops on hook (9 loops on hook). Draw your yarn over the hook and draw it up through 1 loop, *Draw your yarn over the hook and draw through 2 loops. * Repeat from * to * across. The loop which remains on hook always counts as the 1st stitch of next row.

Rows 2 and 3: Insert hook under 2nd vertical bar from the previous row and draw loop through. *Insert hook under next vertical bar from previous row and draw a loop through. *Repeat from * to * across, retaining all loops on hook and working to the last vertical bar. Insert hook through double vertical bar and draw a loop through (thus giving a firm edge to this side). You will have 9 loops on your hook. Draw your yarn over and draw through 1 loop. **Draw your yarn over your hook and draw through 2 loops. ** Repeat from ** to ** across.

Row 4: Make a loop in each vertical bar from the last row until there are 4 loops on hook. Draw your yarn over 3 times, insert hook in 2nd vertical bar on the 3rd row down (into the 1st row) and draw a loop through. (Draw your yarn over and draw through 2 loops) 3 times. Draw your yarn over 3 times, skip 5 bars from the same row and draw a loop through the next vertical bar. (Draw your yarn over and draw through 2 loops) 4 times. This makes a herring bone stitch. Skip the stitch directly behind the herringbone stitch that you just made and make a loop in each of next 4 vertical bars. (there will now be 9 loops on hook.) Draw your yarn over and draw through 1 loop; *Draw your yarn over and draw it up through 2 loops. *Repeat from * to * across.

Row 5: Same as 2nd row. Repeat 4th and 5th rows alternately until piece measures 72 inches long. Sl St in each vertical bar across to finish the row. Fasten off.

Make 2 more strips like this with color A, and sew one on each side of previous strip using Sl St on the wrong sides. Make 2 strips of color B and sew one to side of each previous strip as before. Make 2 strips of color C and sew to previous strips as before. These 9 stripes complete one large strip. Make 2 more large strips like this.

Second Large Strip

With color D make 1 strip. With color D make 2 strips and sew one on each side of previous strip. With color E make 2 strips and sew to sides of previous strips. Wit color F make 2 strips and sew to sides of previous strips. This completes your second large strip. Make one more large strip like this.

Sew your afghan together by alternating between the first large strip and second large strip until all of the strips have been connected. Then, make tassels and attach them to your afghan.

To make your tassels, cut ten 11-inch strands of yarn. Pull strands through center of end of stripe. Form a loop and draw ends through to form a knot. When all fringe has been made, trim it evenly. Your afghan is now done!

Rivers That Ripple Afghan

Beginner.

About:

This rippled afghan features a classic look with beautiful textured waves, and stripes in whichever colors you desire. Due to its nature, this afghan is both cozy and beautiful to look at, making it a wonderful project to spruce up any room, or to offer as a gift to a loved one. The final afghan measures 46 inches by 70 inches.

Materials Needed:

4 weight cotton yarn. 11 skeins of color A, 4 skeins of color B, and 3 skeins of color C. Crochet hook size H.

Abbreviations Used:

Chain (Ch)

Single Crochet (Sc)
Slip Stitch (Sl St)

Pattern:

With color A, Ch 245.

Row 1: Sc in 2nd Ch from hook. Sc in next18 Ch spaces. (3 Sc in next Ch spaces, Sc in next 19 Ch spaces, skip next 2 Ch spaces, Sc in next 19 Ch spaces) 5 times. 3 Sc in next Ch space, Sc in remaining 19 Ch spaces. Ch 1, turn.

Row 2: (In back loop only of each Sc throughout.) Skip first Sc. (Sc in next 19 Sc, 3 Sc in next Sc, Sc in next 19 Sc, skip next 2 Sc) 5 times. Sc in next 19 Sc, 3 Sc in next Sc, Sc in next 18 Sc, skip next Sc, Sc in last Sc. Ch 1, turn.

Row 3 to 8: Repeat 2nd row. Do not Ch 1 at end of 8th row. Drop color A, attach color C. Ch 1, turn.

Row 9: Sc in first Sc. *(Sc in Sc directly below next Sc. Long Sc made,) Skip Sc covered by the long Sc, Sc in next Sc) 9 times. Make a long Sc over next Sc, skip covered Sc, Sc in next stitch, long Sc in same place as last long Sc was made. Point made. (Skip covered Sc. Sc in next Sc, long Sc over next stitch) 9 times. Skip covered Sc, Sc in next 2 Sc. * Repeat from * to * across, ending with Sc in last Sc. Ch 1, turn.

Row 10: With color C, repeat 8th row. Cut and fasten color C. Pick up color A. Ch 1, turn.

Row 11 and 12: Repeat 2nd and 8th rows. Cut and fasten color A, attach color B. Ch 1, turn.

Row 13: With color B, repeat 9th row.

Row 14 to 18: Repeat 2nd row 4 times, then repeat 8th row once. At end of last row cut and fasten color B, attach color A. Ch 1, turn.

Row 19 and 20: Repeat 9th and 8th rows. Cut and fasten color C, pick up color A. Ch 1, turn.

Row 23 to 37: Repeat 2nd row.

Row 38: Repeat 8th row.

Repeat rows 9 through 38 5 more times, then repeat rows 9 through 30 once. Cut and fasten off. Block to measurements. Edging 1st row:

Edging

Row 1: With right side facing, using color A, Sc closely along one long edge. Turn.

Row 2: With wrong side facing, Sl St in each Sc of previous row. Cut and fasten. Work edging along opposite long edge.

Geometric Triangle Afghan

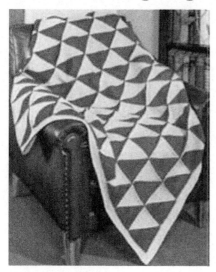

Intermediate.

About:

This geometric afghan is made by creating 108 separate blocks and then sewing them all together to create your afghan. The blanket creates a stunning design that is modern and whimsical, making it wonderful for any home or present. The final blanket is 52 inches by 70 inches.

Materials Needed:

Number 4 weight yarn. 35 balls of color A and 35 balls of color B. Afghan crochet hook size J.

Abbreviations Used:

Chain (Ch)
Single Crochet (Sc)
Slip Stitch (Sl St)

Special Stitch:

Afghan Stitch

Row 1:

Insert hook in 2nd Ch from hook and draw up a loop. Retaining all loops on hook, draw a loop up through each Ch stitch across. There should be 45 loops on your hook now. Yarn over and draw up through 1 loop. *Yarn over and draw up through 2 loops. *Repeat from * to * across until one loop remains on the hook. The one loop will count as your first stitch in your next row.

Row 2:

Insert hook under 2nd vertical bar from previous row and draw a loop through. Retain all loops on the hook as you draw a loop up through each vertical bar across. Yarn over and draw up through 1 loop. *Yarn over and draw up through 2 loops. *Repeat from * to * across until one loop remains on the hook.

Decrease:

To decrease, pass the hook behind two vertical bars on time when you are drawing loops up through your previous row. Then, finish the row as normal.

Pattern:

Block (Make 108)

With color A, Ch 36 to measure 7 ¼ inches.

Work in afghan stitch across, decreasing 1 stitch at both ends of the second row. Decrease by 1 stitch at both ends of the row in every row until three loops are remaining in the row. Yarn over and draw through all three loops. Ch 1 to fasten in your end.

Alongside the opposite end of the starting chain, attach color B and work in afghan stitch across. Decrease 1 stitch at both ends of the second row. Decrease by 1 stitch at both end of the row in every row until three loops are remaining in the row. Yarn over and draw through all three loops. Ch 1 to fasten. Cut and fasten in your end. (Create the exact same block as you made with color A.)

Sew 9 rows of 12 blocks together along the wrong side, with opposite color meeting.

Border

Round 1: Attach color B to one corner. (Sc in each Sc to next corner, 3 Sc in corner Sc.) twice. Cut and fasten off. Attach color A and work other 2 sides in the same border pattern.

Round 2 to 7: With corresponding colors, Sc in each Sc around. 3 Sc in the center of each corner Sc join with Sl St, cut and fasten ends.

Scotch Plaid Woven Afghan

Beginner.

About:

This scotch plaid woven afghan offers brilliant design without being terribly hard for anyone to create. After creating one, you will have great pride in the stunning creation you have made, and people will be surprised that you designed something so wonderful. The final afghan is 58 inches by 72 inches.

Materials Needed:

4 weight yarn. 11 skeins of color A, 19 skeins of color B, 13 skeins of color C, 3 skeins of color D. Crochet hook H. 1 Tapestry needle.

Abbreviations Used:

Chain (Ch)
Single Crochet (Sc)

Double Crochet (Dc)
Slip Stitch (Sl St)

Pattern:

With color C, Ch 219.

Row 1: Dc in the 5th stitch from the hook. *Ch 1, skip 1 stitch of Ch, Dc in next stitch. *Repeat from * to * across row. (108 meshes). Ch 4, turn.

Row 2: Dc in Dc. *Ch 1, Dc in next Dc. *Repeat from * to * across row. Ch 4, turn.

Continue rows of 1 Ch meshes, working 1 more row in color C, then cut yarn.

Attach color B and work 1 row of meses, then work 1 row in color A and 6 rows in color B. *1 row color A, 1 row color B, 3 rows color C, 1 row color B, 2 rows color A, 1 row color D, 2 rows color A, 1 row color B, 3 rows color C, 1 row color B, 1 row color A, 6 rows color B. * Repeat from * to * 4 times. Work 1 more row of color A, 1 row color B and 3 rows color C.

Weaving.

Measure a double strand of color C the length of the afghan. Allow for 10 inches of fringe at each end. Thread the yarn into the tapestry needle. Beginning at the lower right hand corner, weave in and out through the 1st row of meshes on the longest side of the blanket. Take a second double strand of color C and weave in the same row of meshes over the opposite threads.

Continue weaving twice in same meshes with one color in the following scheme: 1 in color C, 1 in color B, 1 in color A, 6 in color B. *1 mesh in color A, 1 mesh in color B, 3 meshes in color C, 1 mesh in color B, 2 meshes in color A, 1 mesh in color D, 2 meshes in color A, 1 mesh in color B, 3 meshes in color C, 1 mesh in color

B, 1 mesh in color A, 6 meses in color B. *Repeat from * to * 3 times. Weave 1 mesh color A, 1 mesh color B, 3 meshes color C. Know fringe close to afghan, knot a second time ½ inch down taking half strands from one knot and half from the next knot.

Two-Tone Blocked Afghan

Beginner.

About:

This beautiful two-toned blocked afghan offers a stunning texture with a two-dimensional color. Based on the design, this afghan can easily be designed to fit into any color scheme as both a subtle yet stunning piece to adorn your room with. This pattern can also be worked up quickly if you are looking for a speedy project to work on. The final size is 51 inches by 62 inches.

Materials Needed:

4 weight yarn. 5 skeins of color A and 5 skeins of color B. (Color A and B should be a darker and lighter tone of the same color.) Crochet hook size H. Blunt end tapestry needle.

Abbreviations Used:

Chain (Ch)
Single Crochet (Sc)
Double Crochet (Dc)

Slip Stitch (Sl St)

Pattern:

One Square

Ch 20. (Ch should measure 5 inches across.)

Row 1: Dc in 4th Ch from hook. Skip 3 Ch spaces. *1 Sc in next Ch, Ch 3, 1 Dc in same Ch, skip 3 Ch. *Repeat from * to * 2 times more. 1 Sc in last Ch, Ch 3, turn.

Row 2: 1 Dc in last Sc of previous row. *1 Sc in next Sc, Ch 3, 1 Sc in same stitch. * Repeat from * to * 2 times more, ending 1 Sc in turning Ch space. Ch 3, turn.

Repeat row 2 nine times more (11 rows). Piece should now measure 4 ½ inches square. Do not cut yarn.

Ch 5, 1 Dc in same stitch, Ch 2. Working down side, space evenly (1 Dc, Ch 2) 4 times. 1 Dc in corner, Ch 2, 1 Dc in same stitch, continue around square in this manner. Cut yarn and fasten.

Make 50 Light Color and 49 Dark Color squares like the one above.

Join squares by sewing them together on the wrong side in alternating colors in rows that are 9 squares long. Sew the lengths together on the wrong side with opposite colors touching until all lengths are attached. The final afghan should be 9 squares wide and 11 squares long.

Border

Attach the darker color in one corner. Work 3 rows of Sc around the afghan, with 3 Sc in each corner to keep the border flat. Cut yarn and fasten.

Bulky Cozy Baby Blanket

Beginner.

About:

This bulky cozy baby blanket is a wonderful chunky, squishy baby blanket that makes for a wonderful gift for any baby, especially a winter baby. Be sure to use a soft baby-appropriate yarn so it is gentle against the baby's skin. The final baby blanket will measure 26 inches by 34 inches.

Materials Needed:

5 bulky weight yarn. 3 skeins of color A, one skein of color B. Crochet hook size J.

Abbreviations Used:

Chain (Ch)
Single Crochet (Sc)
Double Crochet (Dc)

Pattern:

Center

With color A, Ch 61. (About 19 inches across.)

Row 1: Yarn over hook, insert in 3rd stitch from hook, pull up a loop, yarn over hook, skip 1 stitch of Ch. Insert hook through next stitch, pull up a loop, yarn over and pull through all loops at one time. Ch 1. (The ch 1 is termed the eye of the stitch.) *Yarn over hook, insert in same space as the last stitch, pull up a loop, yarn over hook, skip 1 stitch of Ch. Insert in next stitch, pull up a loop, yarn over hook and pull through all loops at one time. Ch 1. * (Pattern.) Repeat from * to * across. Ch 1, turn.

Row 2: Yarn over hook, skip the eye of the last stitch made. Insert hook in next stitch of the same pattern space, pull up a loop, yarn over hook. Insert in eye of the next pattern space, pull up a loop, yarn over and pull up a loop through all loops at one time. Ch 1. *Yarn over hook, insert in eye of the same pattern space, pull up a loop, yarn over hook.

Insert in eye of the next pattern space, pull up a loop, yarn over and pull through all loops at one time. Ch 1. *Repeat from * to * across the row. Insert your hook in the 2nd stitch of the end Ch to complete final pattern. (29 patterns made.) Ch 1 more to turn.

Repeat the 2nd row until piece measures 25 inches. Without cutting yarn, work 80 Sc on each long side and 58 Sc on each short side. Work 3 Sc in each corner to keep project flat. Join, cut yarn, and weave in your ends.

Border

Attach color B in 1st stitch of right corner. Ch 1. Yarn over hook, insert your hook in the same space, pull up a loop, yarn over hook, insert your hook in the next stitch, pull up a loop, yarn over and pull through all loops at one time. Ch 1. *Yarn over hook, insert your hook in the same space, pull up a loop, insert hook in next stitch, pull up a loop, yarn over and pull through all loops at one time. Ch 1. *Repeat from * to * once. *Yarn over hook, insert your hook in the same place, pull up a loop, yarn over hook, skip 1 Sc, insert your hook in next Sc, pull up a loop, yarn over and pull through all loops at one time. Ch 1. *Repeat from * to * all around working the remaining 2 corners the same as 1st corner. Join with a Sl St. Ch 2, turn.

Row 2: Work in pattern same as center section, but increase 1 pattern in each corner. Join with a Sl St, cut color B, turn.

Row 3; Attach color A and work sake as last row.

Row 4: Same as previous row, but increase by 2 patterns at each corner. Cut color A, turn.

Row 5: Attach color B and work same as last row, turn.

Row 6: Same as 2nd row of border.

Row 7: Attach color A and work same as 4th row of border.

Row 8: Work in pattern increasing 1 pattern at each corner. Sl St to join. Cut color A, turn.

Row 9: Attach color B at corner, Sc in same space. *Ch 3, Dc in top of Sc just made. Skip 2 stitches, Sc in next stitches. *Repeat from * to * all around. Sl St to join, but yarn and weave in the ends.

Carriage Cover Baby Afghan

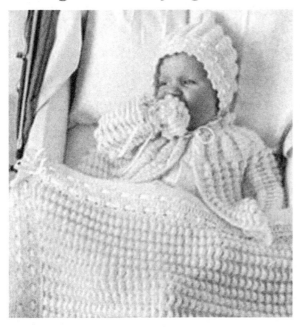

Beginner.

About:

This beautiful carriage cover baby afghan is a double-purpose piece that is wonderful for any new parent, and new baby. The afghan is heavy enough to keep a baby warm, but light enough that it can cover their carriage and keep them protected from the elements without creating too hot of an environment inside of the carriage. It's beautiful texture also makes it a fun blanket for any growing baby to explore the world through.

Materials Needed:

Fingering weight yarn. 6 balls of color C. 9 yards narrow satin. Crochet hook size F.

Abbreviations Used:

Chain (Ch)

Single Crochet (Sc)
Double Crochet (Dc)
Slip Stitch (Sl St)

Pattern:

Ch 125.

Row 1: 1 Sc in 2nd stitch from hook. 1 Sc in each remaining stitch of Ch. Ch 1 to turn each row.

Row 2: Working in back of loop of stitches only. 1 Sc in each of the next 4 Sc. *Ch 1, skip 1 Sc, 1 Sc in each of the next 4 sc. *Repeat from * to * across row.

Row 3: 1 Sc in each of the next 4 sc. *4 Dc in Ch 1, 1 Sc in each of the next 4 Sc. * Repeat * to * across row.

Row 4: Sc in each of the next 4 Sc. *Ch 1, 1 Sc in each of the next 4 Sc. * Repeat * to * across row.

Repeat last 2 rows for pattern until section measures 32 inches.

NEXT ROW: Work 1 Sc in each Sc and in each Ch 1 space.

NEXT ROW: 1 Sc in each Sc. Cut yarn and weave in the ends.

Border:

Attach yarn in any corner stitch.

Round 1: Ch 1, 3 sc in same space. Working in both loops of stitches and all around section, work 1 Sc in each Sc, 1 Sc in each row along each long side working 3 Sc in each corner stitch. Sl St to join in 1st Sc.

Round 2: (Beading) Sl St to corner stitch, Ch 3. Dc in same space. Ch 1, 2 Dc in same space. *Ch 1, skip 1 Sc, 1 Dc in each of the next 2 Sc. *Repeat from * to * to corner. 2 dc, Ch 1, 2 Dc in corner Sc and complete round to correspond. Sl St to join in 3rd stitch of Ch 3 space.

Round 3: Ch 3, 1 Dc in next stitch, 3 Dc in corner stitch, 1 Dc in each Dc and in each Ch 1 around. Work 3 Dc in each corner stitch, Sl St to join in 3rd stitch of Ch 3 space.

Round 4: (Beading) Ch 3, 1 Dc in next Dc, Ch 1, skip 1 Dc, 2 Dc, Ch 1, 2 Dc in next Dc (corner). *Ch 1, skip 1 Dc, 1 Dc in each of the next 2 Dc. *Repeat from * to * around. Work all corners to correspond. Sl St to join in 3rd stitch of Ch 3 space.

Round 5: Ch 1, Sc in same space. Work in back loop of Dc only. 1 Sc in each Dc and in each Ch 1 working 3 Sc in each corner stitch. Ch 1, Sl St to join.

NEXT 3 ROUNDS: Work in back of loop of stitches only. 1 Sc in each Sc. Work 3 Sc in each corner stitch, Sl St to join each round. Cut yarn at end of last round. Lace ribbon through beading and finish each corner with a bow.

Chapter 4:
Patterns With A Purpose

One of the best parts of crocheting is that you can design your patterns to have a wonderful purpose. For example, you can make dish cloths, toaster covers, aprons, and other such patterns that are both stylish and fun to make, while also being useful in many different ways. Once you have been crocheting for a while, being able to create something with purpose is excellent because it allows you to ensure that your craft is both enjoyable and useful. This way, you do not end up with hundreds of afghans and slippers, and no one left to give them to!

Moss Stitch Dish Cloth Pattern

Beginner.

About:

This moss stitch dish cloth pattern is excellent for creating simple dish cloths in any size you want. You can also expand the pattern so that you have tea towels by simply making it twice as long as you would for a dish cloth. They work up in just a few minutes flat, and they work wonderfully even on stubborn messes.

Materials Needed:

4 weight cotton or acrylic yarn. 1 skein in any color. Crochet hook in size H.

Abbreviations Used:

Chain (Ch)
Single Crochet (Sc)
Double Crochet (Dc)
Slip Stitch (Sl St)

Pattern:

Ch 37. (Should be about 5.5 inches across.)

Row 1: In 2nd stitch from the hook, Dc. *Ch 1, skip 1, 1 Dc* across. Ch 2, turn.

Row 2: Dc in space made by previous Ch 1 space. *Ch 1, skip 1, 1 Dc.* Across. Ch 2, turn.

Repeat row 2 until the pattern is as long as it is wide. When you reach the end of the last row, start making your border as follows.

Row 1: Sc 3 times in the corner space. *(Ch 1, skip 1, 1 Sc) evenly across the edge. Sc 3 times in the next corner space. * Repeat from * to * until you have gone all the way around the pattern.

Row 2: Sc 3 times in corner space. *(Ch 1, skip 1, 1 Sc) evenly across the edge. Sc 3 time in the next corner space. *Repeat from * to * around. Cur off the yarn and weave in the ends.

Two-Toned Toaster Cover Pattern

Beginner.

About:

This two-toned toaster cover pattern is a beautiful project that works as a practical piece, too. You can make your toaster cover relatively quickly, and even with the most basic skills. The end result is a piece that will spruce up your kitchen with a vintage feel.

Materials Needed:

4 weight yarn. 4 skeins of color A, 2 skeins of color B. Crochet hook size H.

Abbreviations Used:

Chain (Ch)
Single Crochet (Sc)
Triple Crochet (Tr)

Pattern:

Side piece (Make 2)

Starting at lower edge with color A, Ch 80. (Should measure 11.5 inches.)

Row 1: Tr in 5th Ch from hook, Tr in each Ch across. Ch 4, turn.

Row 2: Skip first Tr, Tr in each Tr across. Ch 4, turn.

Repeat 2nd row until piece measures 4 ½ inches long.

Decrease 1 stitch at both ends of next 3 rows. (Decrease by 1 stitch by working off 2 stitches as 1 stitch.) Decrease 2 stitches at both ends of the next row. Cut off and weave in the end.

Gusset

Starting at lower edge, Ch 40. (Should measure 5 ½ inches.) Work as for side piece without decreasing until piece measures 19 ½ inches. Cur off and weave in ends.

Weaving

Row 1: (Step 1): With right side facing and a single strand of color B, weave over first Tr. *Under 2 Tr, over 2 Tr. *Repeat from * to * across. (Step 2) In same Tr row, weave under first Tr. *Over 2 Tr, under 2 Tr. *Repeat from * to * across. (Step 3) Repeat step 2. (Step 4) Repeat step 1.

Repeat first Weaving Row until all Tr rows are woven. (Be careful to keep continuity of pattern on decrease rows). With color A and right side facing, Sc around side and top edges of both side pieces. Sc across long edges of gusset. Holding side pieces and gusset together and working through both thicknesses, Sc around side and top edges with color A. With color A Sc around lower edge. Sl St join and break off.

Frilly Edged Candy Dish

Intermediate.

About:

This frilly candy dish is a unique piece that offers a delightful texture. It looks as though a doily has been shaped into a dish which can be used to hold individual sweeties or even homemade cookies. If you want to store unwrapped candies or nuts in this dish, place a glass bowl in the center and store them in that.

Materials Needed:

Fingering weight yarn. 2 balls of any color you desire. Crochet hook size J.

Abbreviations Used:

Chain (Ch)
Single Crochet (Sc)
Double Crochet (Dc)
Slip Stitch (Sl St)

Pattern:

Ch 8. Sl St to first Ch to join.

Row 1: Work 15 Dc in ring, Sl St to join.

Row 2: Ch 5. Skip 1 Dc, Dc between next 2 Dc. *Ch 2, Dc between next 2 Dc. *Repeat from * to * around. Ch 2, Sl St to join in 3rd St of Ch 5 space. (15 meshes made.)

Row 3: Sl St into mesh space. Ch 3, 2 Dc in same space. *Ch 2, 3 Dc in next mesh space. * Repat from * to * around. Ch 2, Sl St to join.

Row 4: Ch 5. Skip 1 Dc, Dc in next Dc, *Ch 2, Dc in next Dc, Ch 2, skip 1 Dc, Dc in next Dc. *Repeat from *to * around. Ch 2, Sl St to join in 3rd stitch of Ch 5 space.

Row 5: Sl St into mesh. *Ch 5, thread over needle twice, insert needle in 1st Ch space and pull through, thread over, work off 2 loops twice, thread over needle twice, insert in same stitch, pull through, thread over, work off 2 loops twice, thread over, work off 3 loops. * Repeat * to * skip 1 mesh space, Sc in next mesh. * Ch 5, 2 Tr cluster stitches in 1st Ch, Ch 5, 2 Tr cluster stitches in 1st Ch, Skip 1 mesh space, Sc in next mesh space. *Repeat from * to * around.

Row 6: Sl St on top of petal. *Ch 5, 2 Tr cluster stitches in 1st Ch, Ch 5, 2 Tr cluster stitches in 1st Ch, Sc in top of next 2 petals. *Repeat from * to * around.

Row 7: Sl St on top of petal. *Ch 7, Sc in top between next 2 petals. *Repeat from * to * around.

Row 8: Ch 5, skip 1 stitch, 1 Dc in next Ch space. *Ch 2, skip 1 Ch, 1 Dc in next Ch. *Repeat from * to * around. Ch 2, Sl St to join in 3rd stitch of Ch 5 space. (60 meshes).

Row 9: Same as row 5.

Row 10: Same as row 6.

Row 11: Sl St to top of petal. *Ch 8, Sc in top between next 2 petals. *Repeat from * to * around.

Row 12: Ch 5, skip 2 stitches, Dc in next stitch. *Ch 2, skip 2 stitches, Dc in next stitch. *Repeat from * to * around. (3 meshes made between petals.)

Row 13: Sl St in next mesh space. Ch 3, Dc in same space. *Ch 1, 2 Dc in next mesh. * Repeat from * to * around. Ch 1, Sl St to join.

Row 14: Sl St into next Ch 1 loop. *Ch 5, 2 Tr cluster stitches in 1st Ch space. Ch 5, 2 Tr cluster stitches in 1st Ch, skip the next 2 Dc, loop, 2 Dc, loop, 2 Dc, and Sc in next loop. *Repeat from * to * around.

Row 15: Same a row 6.

Row 16: Same as row 7.

Row 17: 8 Sc in each 7 Ch loop.

Row 18: Ch 4, *1 Dc in next Sc, Ch 1. *Repeat from * to * around. Ch 1, Sl St to join in 3rd stitch of Ch 4 space.

Row 19: Sl St into Ch 1 loop. Ch 5, Dc over next Ch 1 loop. *Ch 2, Dc over next Ch 1 loop. *Repeat from * to * around, Sl St to join.

Row 20: Sl St into Ch 2 loop. *Ch 3, Sc in next loop. *Repeat from * to * around, cut thread.

To Stiffen Your Bowl:

Boil 3 tablespoon of sugar in 4 tablespoons of water for 2 minutes. When it cool, dip the bowl into the syrup, place it over the bottom of a pie dish and smooth it into the shape. Fold the scalloped edges and allow the piece to dry.

Grandma's Traditional Toilet Seat Cover

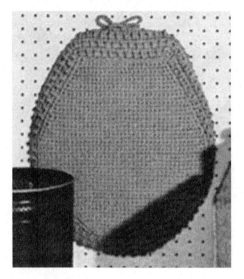

Beginner.

About:

This toilet seat cover will add a touch of decor to your bathroom while also keeping your toilet free of dust. It also adds a tinge of vintage feel to your bathroom, just like grandma's house! This project is excellent for beginners, as it is easy to create though it will expand your skillset so you can take on even more complex projects in the future. Make it in any color you desire to match your bathroom decor, or as a housewarming gift for a loved one!

Materials Needed:

4 weight yarn. 4 balls in any color. Crochet hook in size I.

Abbreviations Used:

Chain (Ch)
Single Crochet (Sc)
Triple Crochet (Tr)
Slip Stitch (Sl St)

Pattern:

Starting at straight edge of center section, Ch 22.

Row 1: Sc in 2nd Ch from hook. Sc in each Ch across. Ch 1, turn.

Row 2: 2 Sc in first Sc (1 Sc increased.) Sc in each Sc to within last Sc, 2 Sc in last Sc (1 Sc increased.) Ch 1, turn.

Row 3: Sc in each Sc across. Ch 1, turn.

Repeat rows 2 and 3 alternately until piece measures 6 inches. Work without increasing for 3 more inches.

Decrease 1 Sc at both ends of the each row until 15 Sc remain. (To decrease by 1 Sc, work through 2 Sc as 1 Sc.) Cut off.

Border

Round 1: Attach yarn to first Sc of first row of center section. 3 Sc in same space. Sc closely around. 3 Sc in last Sc of first row. (End with an even number of Sc.) Sl St to join.

Round 2: Ch 1. *Sc in next Sc, Tr in next Sc. *Repeat from * to * around. Sl St to join.

Round 3: Ch 1. Sc in each stitch around. 3 sc in center Sc of each 3 Sc groups from the previous round. Sl St to Join.

Round 4: Ch 1, *Tr in next Sc, Sc in next Sc. *Repeat from * to * around. Sl St to Join.

Round 5: Repeat round 3.

Round 6: Repeat round 2.

Round 7: Repeat round 3.

Round 8: *Ch 3, skip 2 Sc, Sc in next Sc. *Repeat from * to * around. Sl St to Join and cut off. Fasten in ends.

Make a chain 54 inches long and draw through last round of loops, starting at the flat side of the toilet seat cover. Make a bow there. This will be used to tighten the cover to the seat.

Oval Bath Mat

Beginner.

About:

This simple bath mat pattern is made using cotton yarn. It is advised that you get a rubber no-slip mat to put underneath the rug to avoid accidental slips or falls. This will also help keep the mat from crumpling or folding on the floor when it is being stood on. If you make this mat to match your toilet seat cover, you will have a matching set!

Materials Needed:

4 weight cotton yarn. 6 skeins in any color. Crochet hook number H.

Abbreviations Used

Chain (Ch)
Slip Stitch (Sl St)

Pattern:

Work with two strands at once. Ch 20 (Should measure about 7 inches.) Turn.

Round 1: Insert hook in 2nd stitch from hook, draw loop out on hook. Insert hook in 3rd stitch, draw loop out on hook. Insert in

4th stitch, draw loop out on hook. Insert in 5th stitch, draw loop out on hook. (5 loops on hook.) Yarn over, draw up through all 5 loops at cone. *Ch 1, insert in single loop at back of the Ch just made. Draw loop out on hook, insert hook in outside yarn of stitch just made, and draw loop out on hook. Insert hook in stitch where complete stitch was just made, and draw loop out on hook. Insert hook in next stitch of Ch space, and draw loop out on hook. (5 loops on hook.) Yarn over, and draw up through all 5 loops. *Repeat from * to * until you reach the end of the Ch. Work along other side of foundation Ch.

Round 2: Continue with this same group of stitches for as many rounds as desired. Increases are made at the ends of the mat only. Keep work flat. Increase by making an additional group stitch in the small Ch that fastens the group stitch. As the mat grows in size, more increases as needed at the ends. Work a border of 2 or 3 rounds, using two threads of the same color.

Bumble Bee Striped Oven Mitt Pattern

Beginner.

About:

This oven mitt pattern is a simple pattern that is functional for the kitchen as well. If you stripe it between yellow and black, you get a wonderful bumble bee-like coloring which makes for a whimsical and enjoyable oven mitt. You can also choose to use whatever color stripes you prefer, or create a solid colored oven mitt. Create a pair for a complete set!

Materials Needed:

4 weight yarn in acrylic or cotton. 2 balls of yellow, 1 ball of black. Crochet hook size C. 1 bone ring.

Abbreviations Used:

Chain (Ch)
Single Crochet (Sc)
Slip Stitch (Sl St)

Pattern:

Mitt

Starting at wrist edge with yellow, Ch 21.

Row 1: Sc in 2nd Ch from hook. Sc in each Ch across. Ch 1, turn.

Rows 2, 3, and 4: Sc in each Sc across. Ch 1, turn. At end of 4th row, drop yellow.

Row 5: Attach black to first Sc. Sc in same place and in each Sc across. Ch 1, turn.

Row 6: Sc in each Sc across. Drop black. The first 6 rows establish color pattern.

Row 7, 8, 9, and 10: Pick up yellow. Sc in each Sc across. Ch 1, turn.

Row 11: Sc in each Sc across, 2 Sc in last Sc increased for thumb shaping.) Ch 1, turn.

Row 12: Repeat row 5.

Row 13: Repeat 11th row.

Row 14: Sc in each Sc across to within last 2 Sc, work off 2 Sc as 1 Sc (1 Sc decreased).

Rows 15 and 16: Repeat 13th and 14th rows. Cut off yellow and weave in the ends.

Row 17: Sc in each sc across, 2 sc in last sc. Ch 1, turn.

Thumb

Row 1: Sc in first 6 sc. Turn.

Row 2: Attach yellow to first Sc, Sc in next 4 Sc, 2 Sc in last Sc. Ch 1, turn.

Row 3: Sc in each Sc across. Ch 1, turn.

Row 4: Skip first Sc, Sc in each Sc across, 2 Sc in last Sc. Ch 1, turn.

Rows 5 and 6: Repeat 3rd and 4th rows.

Row 7: Decrease 1 sc at beginning and end of row. Cut off and weave in the ends.

Attach black at base of thumb in the same Sc as last Sc of thumb and continue to work in pattern until 23 rows have been completed.

Row 24: Sc in each Sc, decrease 1 Sc at end of row.

Rows 25, 26, 27, 28, and 29: Work in patterns without decreasing.

Row 30: Sc in each sc across, decreasing 1 sc at end of row.

Row 31: Work without decreasing.

Rows 32 and 33: Repeat last 2 rows. Now decrease 1 Sc at both ends of each row until 8 Sc remain. Cut off and weave in the ends.

Make another piece in the same way.

Holding the two pieces together with the wrong sides out and working through both thicknesses, attach black at the wrist edge. Sc closely around to other side of wrist edge. Cut off and weave in the ends. With black Sc closely around bone ring. Sew ring in place.

Chapter 5:
Advanced Patterns

Graduating from beginner's patterns to advanced patterns is a wonderful opportunity to expand your skills! When you expand from beginner's to advanced, typically the patterns themselves will continue to contain the same stitches that you are already used to, though they will use them in ways that create more advanced results. Here, I have included wonderful patterns that are sure to make you feel like an expert without having to untangle your yarn in a fuss!

Three Little Bears Amigurumi Pattern

Advanced.

About:

These three little bears are the easiest amigurumi teddys you will ever create, and they are absolutely adorable. Their ginormous ears and tiny tufts of hair are sure to capture your heart. Plus, you can play with the bears along to the three little bears nursery rhyme, making it a wonderful present for any child looking for a special present!

Materials Needed:

4 weight yarn. 9 skeins in brown, 9 yards of pink. Crochet hook size J. 24 inch square gold felt. Felt scraps in black, brown, orange, chartreuse, and white. Glue. Filling.

Abbreviations Used:

Chain (Ch)
Single Crochet (Sc)
Slip Stitch (Sl St)

Pattern:

LARGE BEAR

Body:

Ch 5, Sl St to join to form ring.

Round 1: Work 8 Sc in ring, do not join. Place a marker at beginning of each round.

Round 2: 2 Sc in each Sc.

Round 3: Work in Sc throughout, increase to 19 Sc.

Round 4: Increase to 21 Sc.

Round 5: Increase to 29 Sc.

Round 6: Increase to 35 Sc.

Round 7: Increase to 41 Sc.

Round 8: Increase to 48 Sc.

Round 9: Increase to 51 Sc.

Round 10: Increase to 54 Sc.

Round 11: Increase to 58 Sc.

Round 12: Increase to 62 Sc.

Rounds 13 to 33: Work even, cut yarn.

Dividing The Section in Half For Legs

Working through both sections at center only attach yarn in center. Work 1 Sc in 31 Sc around.

NEXT 9 ROUNDS: Work even on the 31 Sc, cut yarn. Attach yarn at center and complete 2nd leg using the same pattern.

ARMS: (Work 2). Work same as body for 3 rounds.

Round 4: Increase to 23 Sc.

Rounds 5 to 12: Work even, cut yarn.

EARS: (Work 2). Ch 10.

Row 1: Sc in 2nd stitch from hook and in each remaining stitches of the Ch.

Row 2: 1 Sc in each Sc.

Rows 3 and 4: Increase 1 stitch in 1st and last stitch.

Row 5: Work even.

Rows 6, 7 and 8: Decrease 1st and last stitch, cut yarn. Attach yarn at corner and work a row of Sc around 3 sides, cut yarn.

MEDIUM BEAR

Work 1st 8 rounds same as Body of Large Bear.

Round 9 through 31: Work even, cut yarn.

LEGS: Divide in half same as Large Bear and work across 24 Sc for each leg for 8 rounds, cut yarn.

ARMS: (Work 2). Ch 5, join.

Round 1: Work 6 Sc in ring.

Round 2: Without joining, work 2 Sc in each stitch.

Round 3: Increase to 15 Sc.

Round 4: Increase to 18 Sc.

Rounds 5, 6, 7, 8, and 9: Work even, cut yarn.

EARS: (work 2). Ch 8.

Row 1: 1 Sc in 2nd stitch from hook and in each remaining stitch of Ch. Ch 10 turn each row.

Rows 2 and 3: Work even.

Row 4: Increase 1 stitch at each end.

Row 5: Work even.

Rows 6 and 7: Dec 1 stitch at each end, cut yarn. Attach yarn at corner and work Sc around 3 sides.

SMALL BEAR

BODY: Ch 5, join.

Round 1: Work 7 Sc in ring.

Round 2: 2 Sc in each stitch.

Round 3: Increase to 17 Sc.

Round 4: Increase to 20 Sc.

Round 5: Increase to 26 Sc.

Round 6: Work even.

Round 7: Increase to 33 Sc.

Round 8: Increase to 36 Sc.

Rounds 9 through 26: Work even, cut yarn.

LEGS: (Work 2). Ch 26, join.

Round 1: Work 1 Sc in each stitch of Ch.

Rounds 2, 3, 4, 5, and 6: Without joining round, work 1 Sc in each Sc, cut yarn.

ARMS: (Work 2). Ch 5, join.

Round 1: Work 6 Sc in ring.

Round 2: 2 Sc in each Sc.

Round 3: Increase to 16 Sc.

Rounds 4, 5, 6, and 7: Work even, cut yarn.

EARS: (Work 2). Ch 6.

Row 1: 1 Sc in 2nd stitch from hook and in each remaining stitch of Ch.

Row 2: Work even.

Rows 3 and 4: Increase in 1st and last stitch.

Row 5: Decrease 1st and last Sc.

Rows 6 and 7: Repeat las row, cut yarn. Attach yarn in corner and work Sc around 3 sides.

FINISHING: Fill body sections with filler.

Use gold felt to fill the inside of your bear's ears, their feet, their hands, and their bellies. Cut eyes and eyelashes from white and black felt and place them on the bear's faces. Use pink yarn to create hair for your bears. To do this, cut the yarn into 2 inch lengths and fold them in half. Pull the fold through the top center of your bear's head and pull the ends through the fold and pull tight for the hair.

Sweetheart Toy Puppy

Advanced.

About:

This adorable puppy pattern is a wonderful pillow-like amigurumi pattern that makes for a wonderful gift for anyone of any age. It features very few details on the face, all of which can be designed using yarn, making it an excellent choice for younger children who may not do well with plastic eyes or accessories on their stuffed animals.

Materials Needed:

4 weight cotton yarn. 2 skeins color A, 1 skein color B. Crochet hook size H. Filling.

Abbreviations Used:

Chain (Ch)
Single Crochet (Sc)
Slip Stitch (Sl St)

Pattern:

PAW: With color A Ch 3.

Row 1: Sc in 2nd stitch from hook, 2 Sc in next stitch of Ch, Ch 1 to turn all rows throughout all sections.

Row 2: 1 Sc in each Sc.

Row 3: Working in Sc increase 1 Sc at beginning and end of row, cut yarn. Set aside.

BODY SECTION: With Natural Ch 3.

Row 1: 2 Sc in 2nd stitch from hook, 2 Sc in next Sc.

Row 2: Working in Sc increase 1 Sc at beginning of row.

Row 3: Increase 1 Sc at beginning and end of row.

Row 4: Repeat row 2.

Row 5: Repeat row 3.

Row 6: Repeat 3rd row.

Row 7: Increase 1 Sc at end of row.

Row 8: 1 Sc in each Sc, Ch 9. Work 1 Sc in each Sc of paw section.

Row 9: 1 Sc in each Sc and in each stitch of Ch.

Row 10: 1 Sc in each Sc.

Row 11: 1 Sc in each Sc.

Row 12: Decrease 1 Sc at end of row. (To decrease: pull up a loop in each of 2 stitches. Yarn over and work off all loops at one time).

Row 13: Decrease 1 stitch at beginning of the row.

Row 14: Decrease 1 stitch at beginning of the row.

Row 15: Increase 1 Sc at beginning of row.

Row 16: Repeat 13th row – 25 Sc.

Row 17: Repeat 12th row.

Row 18: Skip 2 stitches, 1 Sc in each of next 3 stitches. Sl St in each of next 3 Sc, 1 Sc in each remaining stitches.

Row 19: 1 Sc in each of next 14 Sc, decrease 1 stitch, Ch 1, turn.

Row 20: Increase 1 Sc at beginning of row, and decrease 1 Sc at end of row.

Row 21: 1 Sc in each stitch. Repeat last 2 rows once.

Row 22: Repeat row 20.

Row 23: Repeat row 21.

Row 25: Decrease 1 Sc at beginning of the row.

Row 26: Increase 1 Sc at end of row. Ch 3, turn.

Row 27: 3 Sc in 2nd stitch from hook. 1 Sc in next stitch of Ch and in each remaining stitch. 19 Sc.

Row 28: Increase 1 Sc at end of row.

Row 29: 1 Sc in each stitch.

Row 30: Decrease 1 Sc, 1 Sc in each of next 17 Sc, Sl St in next Sc.

Row 31: Skip Sl St, Sl St in next Sc, 1 Sc in each remaining Sc.

Row 32: Decrease 1 Sc, 1 Sc in each of the next 15 Sc, Sl St in next stitch.

Row 33: Skip 1 stitch, 1 Sc in each of next 16 Sc.

Row 34: 1 Sc in each of next 13 Sc, Sl St in each of next 2 Sc.

Row 35: Skip 1 stitch, Sl St in each of next 2 Sc, cut yarn, skip next 3 Sc, attach yarn in next Sc, 1 Sc in each of next 6 Sc, Sl St in each of next 2 Sc.

Row 36: 2 Sc in 1st stitch, 1 Sc in each of next 3 stitches, decrease in next 2 stitches. Ch 1, turn.

Row 37: 1 Sc in each stitch.

Row 38: Repeat row 36.

Row 39: Repeat row 38.

Row 40: 2 Sc in 1st Sc, 1 Sc in each of next 2 Sc. Decrease in next 2 stitches, turn.

Row 41: 1 Sc in each Sc.

Row 42: Repeat row 40.

Row 7: Repeat 2nd row.

Row 8: 1 Sc in each Sc.

Row 43: Repeat row 41.

Row 44: Repeat row 40.

Row 45: Repeat row 41. Cut yarn.

Attach yarn in 1st stitch on opposite side of the Ch between 1st paw and body section. 1 Sc in each of next 7 stitches. Sl St next stitch, cut yarn. Work another section.

EARS: (Make 2). With color B Ch 5.

Row 1: 1 Sc in 2nd stitch from hook and in each remaining stitch of Ch, Ch 1 to turn all rows.

Row 2: Working in Sc increase 1 Sc at beginning and end of row.

Row 3: 1 Sc in each Sc.

Row 4: Repeat 2nd row.

Row 5 and 6: 1 Sc in each Sc.

Row 9: Decrease 1 stitch at beginning and end of row.

Row 10: 1 Sc in each stitch. NEXT 2 ROWS:

Row 11: Repeat 9th row.

Row 12: Repeat 9th row, cut yarn.

EYES: With color B, Ch 2. 4 Sc in 2nd stitch from hook. Sl St to join, cut yarn.

NOSE: Ch 4, cut yarn leaving a length.

FINISHING: Sew 2 sections together leaving an opening for filling. Fill to desired fullness. Sew opening closed. Tack Eyes, Ears, and Nose in position. Embroider Mouth with 2 long stitches.

A Modern Crocheted Apron

Advanced.

About:

This apron pattern is a simple waistband apron that will keep your clothes clean when you are washing the dishes or working in the kitchen. It can also be used in the garden, or anywhere else that you might enjoy wearing an apron. The ruffled pockets make for a truly beautiful piece.

Materials Needed:

4 weight cotton or acrylic yarn. 14 balls of color A and 4 balls of color B. Crochet hook size H. 1 ½ yards of ribbon.

Abbreviations Used:

Chain (Ch)
Single Crochet (Sc)
Double Crochet (Dc)
Slip Stitch (Sl St)

Pattern:

WAISTBAND

With color A, Ch 15 inches long.

Row 1: Dc in 7th from hook, *Skip 3 Ch, in next Ch make Dc, Ch 3 and Dc*. Repeat from * to * across, until piece measure 12 inches long. Cut off remaining chain. Ch 1, turn.

Row 2: Make 4 Sc in each space across. Ch 3, turn.

Row 3: Skip 1st Sc, Dc in each Sc across. Ch 1, turn.

Row 4: Sc in each Dc across and in top stitch of turning chain. Cut off.

Row 5: Attach color B at beginning of last row (right side). Sc in 1st Sc. *Working over next Sc make Sc in the Dc below (long Sc.) Sc in next Sc. *Repeat from * to * across. Cut off. Work along spaces on other side of starting chain to correspond. Cut off.

Hot Springs Bedspread

Advanced.

About:

This bedspread features a delightful lacy-like texture that will add a beautiful feminine glow to your room. It will certainly press your skills into the best possible ones, and because it features repetition it is not as challenging as it may look.

Materials Needed:

4 weight yarn in cotton or wool. 36 balls of yarn in color A. 15 yards of ribbon. Crochet hook size G.

Abbreviations Used:

Chain (Ch)
Single Crochet (Sc)
Double Crochet (Dc)
Slip Stitch (Sl St)

Pattern:

Motif (Make 234.)

Ch 8, Sl St to join to form ring.

Row 1: Ch 1 and work 16 Sc into ring. Sl St to join.

Row 2: Ch 3. *Yarn over, insert in same space with joining. Work off 2 loops. *Repeat from * to * across. Yarn over and work off remaining loops at one time. *Ch 5, skip 1 Sc, cluster stitch in next stitch. (cluster stitch: yarn over, insert in stitch, work off 2 loops, yarn over, insert in same stitch, work off 2 loops, yarn over, insert in same stitch and work off 2 loops twice, then work off remaining 3 loops at one time.) *Repeat from * to * 6 times. Ch 5, Sl St to join.

Row 3: Sl St into next loop. Ch 3 and work a cluster stitch in loop. Ch 4, cluster stitch in same space. Ch 5, Dc in next loop, Ch 5. * 2 cluster stitches with Ch 4 between in next loop. Ch 5, Dc in next loop, Ch 5. *Repeat from * to * around, Sl St to join.

Row 4: Sl St into next loop, Ch 3. **Work 2 cluster stitches with Ch 4 between in 4 Ch loop. *Ch 2, skip 1 stitch of Ch, cluster stitch in next stitch. *Repeat from ** to * 4 times. Ch 2 and repeat from ** around.

Row 5: Sl St into loop. Ch 3 and **Work 2 cluster stitches with Ch 4 between in 4 Ch loop* Ch 2, cluster stitch in next Ch 2. *Repeat from ** to * 5 times. Ch 2 and repeat from ** all around, Sl St to join.

Row 6: Sl St into loop, Ch 3 and **Work 2 cluster stitches with Ch 4 between in 4 Ch loop. * Ch 4, Dc between next 2 cluster stitches. *Repeat from ** to * 6 times. Ch 4 and repeat from ** all around.

Row 7: Sl St to center of loop. Ch 1, 3 Sc over remainder of loop, 4 Sc in each of the next 8 meshes. 3 Sc in corner loop. Ch 9, turn.

Row 8: Sl St over the next Dc of previous row. *Ch 9, skip 1 Dc, Sl St over next Dc. *Repeat from * to * twice. Ch 9, Sl St in 1st Sc in corner loop. Ch 1, turn.

Row 9: *3 Sc over loop, Ch 4, Sl St in top of last Sc for picot, 5 Sc over same loop, picot 3 Sc over same loop. *Repeat from * to * in next 2 loops. 3 Sc, picot, 3 Sc in next loop. Ch 9, turn.

Row 10: Sl St between picots of next scallop, Ch 9, Sl St between picots of next scallop. Ch 1, turn.

Row 11: 3 Sc, picot, 5 Sc, picot, 3 Sc over loop, 3 Sc, picot, 3 Sc over next loop. Ch 9, turn.

Row 12: Sl St between picots of next scallop, Ch 1, turn, 3 Sc, picot, 3 Sc, picot, 3 Sc, picot, 3 Sc over loop, Sl St in last Sc of scallop below and work 2 Sc, picot, 3 Sc over remainder of each of the next 2 loops, 3 Sc, picot, 5 Sc, picot, 3 Sc over next loop, Sl St in top of last Sc in corner and work other 3 sides to correspond.

Chain Mesh Designer Gloves

Advanced.

About:

These dainty designer gloves offer warmth and style. They can be made in any size you desire, and in any color you desire, as well. They make for a beautiful dainty gift for a friend, or as an elegant addition to your own wardrobe.

Materials Needed:

Worsted weight yarn. 1 skein color A , 1 skein color B. Crochet hook size J.

Abbreviations Used:

Chain (Ch)
Single Crochet (Sc)
Double Crochet (Dc)
Slip Stitch (Sl St)

Pattern:

Forefinger, Middle Finger, Ring Finger and Little Finger

Round 1: 7 Sc in ring (do not join but continue as spiral.) Sc in Ch 1 space.

Rounds 2 and 3: Sc in each Sc.

Round 4: *Ch 3, skip Sc, Sc in next. *Repeat from * to * 3 more times. (4 Ch 3 loops made.)

Round 5: *Ch 3, Sc in next ch 3 loop. * Repeat from * to * until finger is desired length. Make fingers slightly shorter than actual finger so they fit better.

Thumb.

Ch 4, Sl St to form ring. Ch 1.

Round 1: 9 Sc in ring (do not join but continue as spiral.) Sc in Ch 1 space.

Rounds 2 and 3: Sc in each Sc.

Round 5: *Ch 3, Sc in next ch 3 loop. *Repeat from * to * until thumb is desired length.

Palm.

Lay fingers in order, and join one mesh of one finger to one mesh of other with over and over stitches. Fasten thread to outside of little finger.

Round 1: *Ch 3, Sc in next Ch 3 loop, *Repeat from * to * across palm, and continue across back of hand. Do not join, but continue as a spiral.

Round 2: *Ch 3, Sc in next Ch 3 loop, *Repeat from * to * around and around up to the thumb. Now try glove on and mark place for thumb- Sew 2 meshes of thumb to 2 meshes of glove.

Continue with pattern, working over the glove and the thumb for 6 rounds.

For the next round, decrease 1 mesh at beginning of thumb and 1 mesh after working over 3 meshes of thumb to decrease a mesh, after Ch 3 is made, Sc in next loop and then Sc in next loop).

Continue is spiral as far as writs, ending at little finger side of wrist.

Cuff.

Row 1: Attach colored yarn to finishing stitch of glove. Ch 2, Dc in same Ch 3 loop. * Sc in next Ch 3 loop, Ch 2, 3 Dc in same Ch 3 loop. *Repeat from * to * to end of row. Do not join. Ch 2, turn.

Row 2: Sl St in Ch 2 loop of last shell made. Ch 2, 3 Dc in same Ch loop as Sl St was made. *Sl St in Ch 2 loop of next shell, Ch 2, 3 Dc in same Ch loop as Sl St was made. *Repeat from * to * to end of row. Ch 2, turn.

Rows 3 to 8: Same as 2nd row. After completing 8th row, cut off. Turn.

Row 9: Attach color A in last Dc made. In Ch 2 loop made at beginning of last shell, make 1 Sc, 2 Dc, 1 Sc. *In Ch 2 loop of next shell, make 1 Sc, 2 Dc, 1 Sc. *Repeat from * to * to end of row. Fasten off. Weave in ends.

Printed in Great Britain
by Amazon